Always & Forever

Michael Cory

BookLeaf Publishing

India | USA | UK

Presentation by *BookLeaf Publishing*

Web: www.bookleafpub.com

E-mail: info@bookleafpub.com

ISBN: 9789363318489

First edition 2024

To the love of my life, both past, present, and future.

Without your unwavering belief in me, this would still be a mere thought tucked away in some forgotten corner of my mind.

Thank you, my love, for all your unwavering encouragement, inspiration, and persistence. Your belief in me has been the driving force behind my journey, and I am forever grateful for that!

From the bottom of my heart,

through the depths of my soul

I will always love you,

I will always choose you,

In every lifetime.

Always and Forever

ACKNOWLEDGEMENT

Poetry is a language,
that tells us through more or less emotional
reaction,
something which cannot be said.

Edward Arlington

PREFACE

Last night I had a wonderful dream. I dreamt I was in a never-ending
fog. Though at first, it was not so wonderful.
I was wandering around unquestioningly. I was searching for
something I did not even know.
Every face I saw was estranged, zipping here and there past me,
Appearing only to evaporate before my very eyes back into the fog. But in the darkest and loneliest moment, I saw a face shining brighter than any star in the heavens.
I saw the face of someone who has been a part of my life for an eternity. Your eyes, speaking to me with a softness and gentleness that rivals the warm summer breeze of the lake, seemed to smile at me, inviting and calming. In that moment, I knew, there was no one else like you.
Such an angelic face that stood out from the rest.
I could not believe I finally found you after searching without knowing you.
You extended your hand and whispered take it. Everything will be OK, trust me and take my hand. You will be safe and sound, wrapped in the warmth of our love.

I'll lead you out of this dark and lowly place.

Then, as I laid my hand in yours, we flew up towards the heavens above the clouds, hurtling towards the brightest star, twirling around and around like two sparrows caught in a cosmic embrace. We were not just happy but blissful and deeply in love. Then I woke up and realized that this was no dream. I had been presented with the truth. Please take me up, my fiery angel, my beloved sparrow, and let us continue this journey of joy and love together.

Wherever your path leads, I am not just willing, but eager to walk it with you. Your journey is mine, and I am here to support you, always.

Please stay by my side forever and complete me. My eyes, my eyes need to see what you see. My ears need to hear what you hear. My soul needs to feel the warmth of your embrace.

I recognize now that you are God's extraordinary gift of love.

I have loved you through all the sunshine and the downpour.

While I may sometimes say it all too often, I want you to know that I love you with every fibre of my being. You are not just my partner but my best friend, the most adorable, strong-willed, wonderful, and caring individual I have ever known.

My love, you give meaning to life itself. It has been a credit to have you as an everlasting friend, lover, mother, and especially today and every day after, standing beside me for all eternity as my wife.

Every day, your love binds me more deeply than I knew the day before. So, no day is the same now, but each one is a little happier than the last.

My own, you are MY very own, and yet true as that may be, it is not so true as that I am YOUR own. It is less absolute and must be so because I cannot take possession of anything when given over my heart and soul.

There isn't enough identity left in me.

I am yours, and all of this is useless for you to know.

I will always love and cherish you. Till our very last breath and beyond the stars that light up the heavens of every lifetime we find each other in. You are my only shining star.

On this day, I vow to you my eternal love in sickness and health and my unwavering dedication to our relationship. All my love is yours and yours alone. I promise to be by your side, supporting and loving you, for all the days of our lives.

I hope and pray this fairy tale you have made my life stay and that we're good friends to the end, in our minds, bodies, and spirits.

I love you with all my heart and soul. I love you far, far beyond my control. I always will because what we share is more beautiful than the colours of any rainbow, for they will never fade in days or only appear in or after the rain.

I love the feeling of happy tears rolling down my face. I love the taste of you when we kiss because it's an everyday sweetness—it's meek and willing.

You've made my ending a new beginning.

There are no other words to pen this scary commentary,

That I am sharing with you and everyone right now,

but I will say this again and again, time after time, Elephant Shoe!!!

Tears For Tula

In a little farmhouse tucked away so small,
Lived a tortoiseshell cat with a heart to enthrall.
She was gentle as a whisper,
bright as a morning star,
Oh, Tula, you brought love from near and far.

On summer evenings, she'd curl into our lap,
With every purr, she'd leave her soft, wet map.
Drooling love like rain, her own gentle way,
Tula's little kisses brightened every day.

Oh Tula, Tula, now where have you gone?
Your absence has left a void, a silence that
echoes in our hearts.
The hearth feels cold, and the nights are long.
Our hearts are heavy, like the morning dew,
We miss the love you gave, simple and true.

From dawn 'til dusk, she painted our world,
With tiny wet footprints, our lives unfurled.
In the fields and meadows, she chased
butterflies,
Now, we look for her in the open skies.

Oh Tula, Tula, now where have you gone?

Our yearning for your presence grows with each
passing day.
The hearth feels cold, and the nights are long.
Our hearts are heavy, like the morning dew,
We miss the love you gave, simple and true.

The rocking chair's still swayin', but it's missing
a friend,
Our hearts are torn; will they ever mend?
We place your favourite blanket by the firelight,
Hoping somehow, you'll come back tonight.

Lonely Bean

Yodelin' down the dirt road, found a bean sittin'
all alone
There's no crew, just green and mean; man, this
bean's in a zone
Stuck in life's gumbo, ain't got no chilli kin
Rustlin' in the breeze, singin' a desolate hymn

Hillbilly heartbreaks put a spin on this tale
Bean's soliloquy, strong yet incredibly frail
Fermented dreams bubbling in cowboy steel
pots
Lonely rides, while the sunset shots connect dots

Lonely bean, driftin' on life's prairie
Rhythms of sorrow couldn't get more scary
A lone sagebrush in a field of weeds
Groovin' to misery on dusty back roads and
leads

Swingin' between barn walls, moonlight
whiskey in tow
This lonesome legume got flow dipped in those,
you know?
Campfire tales, voices hidden in the smoke
Rootless existence, country dividends revoke

Guitar twang strums, old cowboy stories hum
Bean reminisces back when he had a chum
Rattlesnake fight night, midnight starlit skies
Cowpoke's life dwindles in his lonely eyes

Little Man Under the Hood

Engine purrs, rhythm and blues,
Tiny dude, keepin' it smooth—grease-stained
shoes.
Wrench in hand, fast moves like a roadrunner,
Pistons fire; he is the real heart-thumped.

Oil and grime, he was a mechanical wizard,
Big truck, small stature, metaphorical blizzard.
Knows the crankshaft like a mother knows her
child,
Fixing up rigs with a damn devilish smile.

Little man under the hood, making magic like
Merlin,
Turn a rust bucket into a Florida whirlwind.
Every bolt, every nut, you know he understood,
Hittin' highways—he's the little man under the
hood.

Country dirt roads, hip-hop flow,
Tiny town hero, everybody knows.
Rev the engines, feel the rumbling thunder,
Little guy wrenching never makes you wonder.

Hands like steel, but a heart of solid gold,

Fix up your Chevy, even if it's old.
Country tunes on the radio, rap beat in his mind,
A small-town mechanic, working overtime.

Lil' Grease Monkey

Under that hood, Lil Man with the wrench,
Jump-start dreams, oil-stained trench,
Dust bunnies floatin', engine heart poundin',
He tightens bolts, whole world spinnin' round
him.

Rustbelt anthem, echo from the garage,
Grease Monkey anthem, distorted collage,
Gritty fingers dance, steel-toed ballet,
Pistons poppin', darkness into day.

Lil' man under the hood takin' no flack,
Gasoline veins runnin' the track,
Wrench warrior, ain't backin' down,
King of the chains, wearin' that crown.

Broken down dreams, Detroit cold steel,
No college degree, but I got a tough deal,
Fixin' up Corvettes, NASCAR fantasies,
Beneath the hard hat, sculptin' his masterpiece.

Cheered on by the roar of midnight streams,
Torque's teacher, Metal Sheen, dreams,
Beneath fluorescent lights, let the world
misunderstand,
Lil' man fixes and turns the wrench with both
hands.

Green-Eyed Clover

In the land of green hills, she's my four-leaf
clover,
Red-haired magic with freckles, pure Casanova,
Boots hit the ground, dirt roads under cover,
Whistlin' tunes, heartbeats sweet as Kentucky
butter.

I found her in the pub, a Guinness drinker, not a
fighter,
Gypsy soul dances, the night a little brighter,
Shamrock smiles; no other can inspire,
She's a hurricane of love, Irish fire.

She's my pretty little Irish girl, oh yeah,
Green-eyed beauty, a world in a twirl, declare!
Leprechauns haven't found gold; it's her.
Beware,
Whiskey flows; true love we share is rare.

Fiery temper, sweeter than molasses,
Wildflower blooms, ev'ry town she passes,
Celts carved her grace, song for the masses,
On her lips whispers secrets, ancient classes.

Fiddles play her tune, barns rock a ballad,

Her presence, a melody, is never to be forgotten.
Kisses in clover fields, fear be invalid,
Rainbow's end in her eyes, a tale so candid,
Heart's treasure chest, she's the bandit.

Deez Nuts on the Range

Cowboy boots scuffed, dust risin' on the plains,
Deez nuts swingin' heavy, ain't no ball and
chain,
Campfire sizzles, beans bubblin' in the pot,
But you, who's the cowboy without deez nuts
hot?

Ridin' down the dusty trail, hear the cattle bawl,
Lasso in one hand, and deez nuts going to call,
Spit shine on my buckle, spurs catchin' in the
light,
In every saloon, deez nuts the talk of the night.

Deez nuts on the range, can't be tamed, can't be
locked,
You all can bet your boots, deez nuts rock,
Weatherin' storms like an actual country stock,
Deez nuts on the range, around the clock.

Coyote howl, moon's up, deez nuts in the breeze,
Roughriders know you don't touch Deez without
a please,
Whisky in my flask, raspy voice begins to croon,
Tales of deez nuts leadin' every round-up tune.

Kickin' dust with every boot stomp, tellin' tales so grand,
Cowpoke chatter echo, deez nuts rule the land,
From the barn to the bar, ain't a soul can run,
Deez nuts, the legend starts wrestling the sun.

Beach Party

The white sands on my toes
Sunshine on my face
Bikinis and wet t-shirts
We're dancing all over the place

Corona in my hand
Laughter in the air
Dirt roads lead us here
We have no worries or cares

In the bed of a truck
We're feeling so free
Singing along to old tunes
Under the summer breeze

Beach parties under the stars
Guitars strum the night
Bonfire lighting hearts
 And Everything feels alright

Waves crashing on the shore
Friends gathered all around
Memories forevermore
Here in this beach town

In the bed of a pick-truck
We're feeling so free
Singing along to old tunes
Under the summer breeze

Beach parties under the stars
Guitars strum the night
Bonfire lighting hearts
And everything feels alright

Waves crashing on the shore
Feels so sweet

Beach parties under the stars
Guitars strum the night
Bonfire lighting hearts
And everything feels alright

Forever & a Day

Saturday night at the honky-tonk
Good folks living like they can't be wrong
Cold beer in hand, And the band's playing strong
A love of a woman where my heart belongs [

Old Joe's spinning tales by the jukebox light
Betty Lou's got a smile so bright
Laughter fills the air
We're feeling right
Holding you close
Dancing through the night

Good folks
Cold beers
Love that's here to stay
Beneath the neon glow
We're making our way
Hand in hand
We'll find our place
Together forever and a day

Sunrise with you by my side
Morning coffee
Sweet country pride
In your eyes

I see my guide
Down this road
I'll never hide

Kids playing in that summer breeze
Future's bright
Like the tall oak trees
Family's love
Puts my mind at ease
Living life just as we please

No More Tula

Tula's chirp in the morning light
Drooled with love like stars so bright
Empty bowl, quiet house, cold
Her warmth gone, stories untold

Once purring near the window still.
Now echoes haunt when the night is still
Tortoiseshell beauty eyes so wise
Gone too soon under pale skies

Tula, oh, where'd you go
Why'd you leave this sorrow
Love poured out without restraint
Memories now only paint

She'd curl 'round in gentle sleep.
Now, her loss is all I keep
Every corner whispers her name
Life without her not the same

I look to the stars at night
Seeking comfort in their light
To hold her once more, if I may
In dreams where shadows play

Tula, oh, where'd you go
Why'd you leave this sorrow
Love poured out without restraint
Memories now only paint

Tula, oh, where'd you go
Why'd you leave this sorrow
Love poured out without restraint
Memories now only paint

Sunday Supper

In a small town kitchen, there's a heart made of
flame,
Where the scent of roast beef puts big city
shame.
Mama stirs the gravy, and Dad carves with
cheer,
In the heart of this house, love's always near.

Potatoes are mashed, and the rolls rise high,
Grandma's old recipes never passed by.
Cousins are laughing, stories are told,
And that roast beef's tender, just like spun gold.

Roast beef, roast beef, brings us all together,
From summer sun to cold winter weather.
Around this table, we find our peace,
Blessings are shared with each slow-cooked
piece.

Little one's eyes wide, awaiting their first bite,
Holidays or Sundays, it always feels right.
Smiling through the chatter, hearts full and
bright,
Roast beef is our tradition every single night.

On the stove is a pot of green beans, just
steamed,
With a dollop of butter, like Granny had
dreamed.
Cornbread is crumbling, sweet tea in the glass,
As we savour the moment, let the good times
last.

And when life gets tough and roads seem too
steep,
With a dollop of butter, like Granny had
dreamed.
Cornbread is crumbling, sweet tea in the glass,
As we savour the moment, let the good times
last.

And when life gets tough and roads seem too
steep,
We know where to turn, where comfort runs
deep.
it's the meals that we share, the love that
remains,
With each bite of roast beef, you can forget all
your pains.

And when life gets tough and roads seem too
steep,
With a dollop of butter, like Granny had
dreamed.

Cornbread is crumbling, sweet tea in the glass,
As we savour the moment, let the good times
last.
As we savour the moment, let the good times
last.
 And when life gets tough, it brings us all
together.

Heart of the Glen

There, in the heart of the Glen
So wild
I watched the stars with my youngest child
Beneath the old oak tree
Our shelter true
I sang the songs that my father knew

Her eyes sparkled like the morning dew
With giggles light
The sky seemed new
Her tiny hand in mine
A perfect fit
Love's deep well in this quiet bit

O
My heart
Forever bound
In the echoes of laughter
Love Profound
Through the winds and the whispers of the glen
My children
My world
Till the very end

My son

With dreams as vast as the sea
Climbed hills and valleys
Wild and free
A warrior's heart
Yet gentle and kind
Strength of the mountain
Spirit unconfined

In shadows, long and twilight's glow
We carve the memories
And time moves slow
The fireside tales and whispered songs
Bind us tightly where we belong

He Taught Me How to Dream

Sunrise over the fields
He stood tall and proud
Calloused hands
Gentle eyes
Not much was loud
Knew every corner
Every whisper of the land
Taught us love in the silence
And to always stand

Passed down the stories like a river flowing
behind
Of mountain dreams
Of trials
Of an unwavering mind
In the barn and the garden
Where the summers bled gold
Thrived lessons in patience
And a spirit bold

He taught me how to dream.
With calloused hands
So true
The world before my eyes
Through skies, we never knew

With silent strength and love always near
In every step I take
He's whispering clear

Old leather boots
And a weathered brim so wide
Beneath them, I saw the world and the far and
wide
In the simple acts of working
He showed what's real
Brought dreams to a land
Taught a heart to heal

Father's lullabies in the dusk of open skies
With each note
Faith and hope would rise
Showed me stars in the quiet of the night
And in their glow
His love was my light

Deez Nuts

Rollin' through the heartland, cowboy hat tip
I got a sack of peanuts and a joke on my lip
I need no saddle; I got my truck well-steady
Skies lookin' sunny, and the jokes comin' ready

Deez nuts got the whole town singin'
From the barn to the bar, laughter ringin'
Kickin' up dust in our cowboy boots
Crackin' up the crowd about deez nuts, no
disputes

Out on the ranch, horses all a-strut
Even they are smilin' about Deez nuts
Neighbours stop by, wanna hear the same joke
Granny laughs so hard nearly has a stroke

Deez nuts got the whole town singin'
From the barn to the bar, laughter ringin'
Kickin' up dust in our cowboy boots
Crackin' up the crowd about deez nuts, no
disputes

Rodeo nights, bonfire glow
Crack another joke, and the crowd's ready to
blow

From the corral to the old saloon, holler
Even the old sheriff can't help but waller

Life's simple pleasures in a small-town scene
Livin' for the moments, you know what I mean?
A good laugh heals straight from the gut
On the tip of your tongue, it's always deez nuts

Sunrise on the Lakes

Sunrise on the shadows of the lake stretch too long Morning mist breath slow colours pour in dawn Reflections dance on water sighs are finally gone Northwestern Ontario where time feels like a song.

The dandelions, their heads stung by frost, whisper in the autumn air. The leaves, now amber-red, lead me into the season. The fishing boats, drifting idle, are fed by nature's dreams. As the sunset wraps me tight, I feel warm in the cold bed of the night.

The rising sun burns fear; low it goes again. Lakes embrace the stories cast from men's hands. Then, Walk the shores alone or find a new old friend. Seasons change, and our hearts rise and fall. Come see where it ends.

Summer in Northwestern Ontario feels like freedom as I walk barefoot on the fire. The silent nights, adorned with star shine, lift my soul higher. The echoes of laughter, singing with the lakeside choir, fill the air. In the blink of the weather's eye, dreams never tire

Winds that blow through trees tell tales untold
Crisp and cutting cold warmth that once they
hold Journey's just beginning seasons fill the
fold Nature's gentle whispers this story now
unfolds.

Spring revives the sleeping hearts trapped
beneath the snow. Creaking ice is crackling
under the sunshine's glow. Water, like a mirror,
reveals all we need to know. Lakes of
northwestern Ontario forever you'd bestow

Boots & Beats

DJ hollerin', spinnin' steel horses,
Cowgirl boot tap, DJ star endorses,
Hay bale benches, in a barn ball so brassy,
Kick drum thumpin', boots so sassy,
Twangin' guitars, beats bumpin' steady,
Crowd roarin' louder, DJ hands ready.

City slicker mix, wild hoedown breeze,
Turntables scratchin', banjo strings ease,
Wranglers stompin', dance floor crazy,
Neon lights flash, cowpoke hazy,
Swing ya' partner, fill the barn wide,
Boot scoot boogie, DJ be your guide.

Floor packed, yeehaw roars,
DJ JacD, bringin' dance galore,
Boots clack, jumpin' on planks,
Turn up the track, give the DJ thanks,
Night ignites, rhythm takes control,
Country rap, heart and soul.

Elbow grease track, bar doors slam wide,
Cornfield row beats spread worldwide,
Vinyl spin spark, in this barn so deep,
Whisky shots fire, DJ's creek they'll reap,

Twang n' bass dropping, fillin' homes with pride,
Amplified heartbeat, DJ, our guide.

Steel strings ring beats pounding pure,
Dust cloud rising, wild west allure,
Cowpoke hat down, shadows on the floor,
DJ swings this barn, leave 'em wantin' more.

Coffee Shop Cutie

I strolled into the cafe, boots clickin' on the tiles,
She had a smile like sunshine; it stretched for
country miles,
Pourin' out my java, sayin' "cream and sugar
too?"
Her laughter rang like church bells. Lord, what
am I gonna do?

She's got a sassy apron with stains from days
gone by,
But she brews a pot of magic, makes me feel
like I can fly,
I tried to drop a line, somethin' witty, somethin'
grand,
But all that came out was, "Hey there, can I lend
a hand?"

Oh, coffee shop cutie, makin' hearts skip a beat,
You stir my lonely mornings with your laughter
and your heat,
If love were caffeinated, I'd be bouncing off the
walls,
Oh, coffee shop cutie, in your arms is where I
fall.

She's got a way with muffins that keeps me comin' back,
It ain't just about the sweets, it's the way she makes 'em stack,
Cinnamon and sugar, oh, those freckles on her face,
I'm dreamin' 'bout her lovin', ain't no need for corporate chase.

Once she caught me starin', she raised a brow and laughed,
I said, "I ain't just drinkin', darling, I'm fuelin' up my craft,"
She poured me one on the house, winked and walked away,
Now I'm strummin' on my guitar, singin' 'bout her every day.

Smooth as Silk

Down in the holler where the moonshine flows,
There's a man named Billy, everyone knows,
He's smoother than the whisky that he brews in
his still,
Just like satin threads, he's got some serious
skill.

Got a shirt so slick it can blind the sun,
Bought it off a peddler for a gallon of rum,
He says it's made from the clouds up high,
When Billy walks by, you can only sigh.

He's smooth as silk, yeah, makes the ladies
swoon,
Like a hot knife through butter cuts the
afternoon,
When he's around, the world's a funnier place,
With a silk-lined hat and a smile on his face.

He slides into town like a dream in the night,
Wearing all his finery, what a sight,
They say he's got a stash of that silky thread,
Hidden in his barn, right under his bed.

But the sheriff doesn't mind; he's a friend of
Bill's,
Even I asked him for a pair of silky frills,
Cause when you're wrapped in silk, everything's
alright,
Whether chasing bandits or holding hands tight.

One Foot Out the Door

I saw her first by the old town store,
Sunset in her eyes, heart wanting more.
She walked like she had somewhere to be,
With a tiny suitcase and dreams running free.

We'd talk all night on her front porch swing,
I'd play the guitar, she'd laugh and sing.
But every night, she'd say "I gotta be movin' on,"
With one foot out the door, before the dawn.

She's a wildflower in the wind, never staying too
long,
Chasing distant melodies, writing her own song.
With one foot out the door, she keeps me
wanting more,
But I can't pin her down, she's a love I can't
ignore.

We'd dance under the pale moonlight,
I'd hold her close, but she'd always take flight.
Love was a fleeting fire in her eyes,
Always burning bright, but ready to rise.

She'd talk about cities she's never seen,
Dreams painted on a canvas of green.

I'd say, "Stay a while and be my girl,"
But she'd just smile, lost in her own world.

Coffee Shop Crush

Stumbled in this mornin' eyes feelin' heavy
Guitar on my back nerves run steady
Handed me a latte smile so wide
Caught me off guard and took me for a ride

Hey, coffee shop cutie got me feelin' so alive
Your eyes are so blue, like the morning sky
Heartbeats race. You're my caffeine high.
Hey, coffee shop cutie, let's take a wild ride.

Every day, I see you behind that counter
Life's a blur, but you standin' there, I'm brighter
Swear, sometimes you glance my way
I want to say hi, but words fade away

Fantasy dreams of us dancin' in the dark
Feel your touch like a lightning spark
Timidly, I asked if she would understand
Just a country boy's heart in my hands

Got the courage said Hey, what's your name
The smile widened, said Lucy, caught in the
flame
We talked all night under that neon light
Coffee shop cutie, my soul took flight

Every day, I see you behind that counter
Every day, I see you behind that counter

Rollin' in the Hay

Sunset's falling low
A cool breeze starts to blow
Out on this dusty road
Gonna find some fun tonight

Cold beer in my hand
Country gals in a band
Trucks rolling 'across the land
Feeling free and light

We're Rock and rollin' in the hay.
Under the moonlight, we will sway.
Laughter echoes far away.
And I don't have any worries here.

Fields stretch out so wide,
bathed in the golden hues of the setting sun.
Bleachers where we'll hide
Stars shining in their pride
I love to be right here

Engines start to rev
Dancing 'til we sweat
Music's playin' loud
Feelin' alive and proud

Wilderness Symphony

Moose stompin' round the great white north
Beaver is busy with its wooden fort
Loons cryin' a tune along the shore
Echoes through the night can't be ignored

Bear in the forest diggin' for gold
Wolf howlin' tales of days of old
Caribou runnin' through the snow
Nature's Orchestra a wild show

Lakes of the north where the wild things play
Singin' under skies both night and day
Creatures from mountains to the shores
Canada's heartbeats rock forevermore

Eagle soarin' high among the trees
Fox playin' tricks bringin' the breeze
Otter on its back rollin' in the lake
Northern lights above nature's own shake

Spirit of the land whispers to the wind
Stories in the night are never going to end
Echoes through the lakes and forests deep
Secrets that the wild will always keep

On the canoe driftin' past it all
From the tiny critters to the majestic tall
Life in every corner can't constrain
Canada's wild spirit can't contain